A FUNNY THING
HAPPENED ON THE WAY
TO THE FUTURE

A FUNNY THING HAPPENED ON THE WAY TO THE FUTURE

Twists and Turns and Lessons Learned

MICHAEL J. FOX

HYPERION

NEW YORK

Library of Congress Cataloging-in-Publication Data
has been applied for.

ISBN: 978-1-4013-2386-8

Hyperion books are available for special promotions and
premiums. For details contact the HarperCollins Special
Markets Department in the New York office at 212-207-7528,
fax 212-207-7222, or email spsales@harpercollins.com.

Book design by Karen Minster

FIRST EDITION

10 9 8 7 6 5 4 3 2 1

THIS LABEL APPLIES TO TEXT STOCK

We try to produce the most beautiful books possible, and
we are also extremely concerned about the impact of our
manufacturing process on the forests of the world and the
environment as a whole. Accordingly, we've made sure
that all of the paper we use has been certified as coming
from forests that are managed to ensure the protection
of the people and wildlife dependent upon them.

For all of my teachers.

Contents

Contents

A FUNNY THING HAPPENED ON THE WAY TO THE FUTURE

FINALLY . . . THE BEGINNING

MY PURPOSE IN WRITING THIS BOOK IS NOT TO OFFER advice. Sure, I make the occasional suggestion, mostly common sense stuff. If it works, feel free to work it, though chances are you'll figure this out on your own. If anything, this is a book that tells you that you don't need a book. That is, you don't need a book to tell you what you need. What I've done here is draw a few observations based on my life experience and organize them in response to the broader question: *What constitutes an education?* Have the last dozen-plus years prepared you for the future? Obviously, that's impossible for you or anyone to know. I could spend five months poring over your transcript and I still wouldn't be able to predict what the next five minutes have in store. Life is a ride. Strap in, hang on, and keep your eyes open.

A friend of mine shared this story with me. It's a parable, origin unknown, and I found resonance in its simple truth.

.   .   .

A PROFESSOR STANDS before his class with a cardboard box. From inside he produces a large, clear, empty pickle jar, and then a series of golf ball-sized rocks, which he then drops one by one into the jar until they reach the brim.

"So?" the teacher asks. "Who thinks the jar is full?" Hands shoot up, and a quick scan of the room confirms unanimity—yes, it's full.

Next out of the box, a bag of sand, which the professor pours in amongst the rocks. Tiny grains cascade over, around, and in between the larger stones until there is no space left.

"Is it full now?" A show of hands and a chorus of voices responds—yes, it's full.

Now the professor smiles. "But wait." Both hands disappear into the box and reemerge simultaneously, each holding a can of beer. The crack and hiss of the pop tops are drowned out by laughter in the classroom as the amber nectar pours into the jar with the rocks and sand. Once the din of the students subsides to a collective chuckle, the professor confidently declares, "Now it's full."

"This jar represents your life," he continues. "Make sure the first ingredients are the big stuff . . . the rocks— your family, your work, your career, your passions. The rest is just sand, minutiae. It's in there. It may even be important. But it's not your first priority."

"What about the beer?" a kid in the back yells out.

"Well," comes the answer. "After everything else, you always have room for a couple of beers with friends."

.　　.　　.

I THOUGHT ABOUT saving the metaphor of the jar and the stones for the conclusion of this book, but I wanted to pass it on to you as quickly as possible. You now know what it took me decades to learn. Among other things, don't start with the beer.

Let me explain . . .

PART I

Two Schools

"I've never let my schooling
interfere with my education."

MARK TWAIN

MY PHOTO APPEARED ON THE MAY 23, 2008, FRONT PAGE
of my hometown paper, the *Vancouver Sun*, but the head-
line identified me as "Dr. Michael J. Fox." As neither I
nor my brother, Steve, had ever given our mother any reason to expect that she'd someday utter the words "my son
the doctor," she was immensely proud that the University of
British Columbia had pronounced her baby boy a "Doctor
of Laws."

Would it be crass to mention that I also have a doctorate of Fine Arts from NYU, as well as a doctorate of

Humane Letters from Manhattan's Mt. Sinai School of Medicine? They're honorary, of course, which puts me on equal academic footing with the Scarecrow from *The Wizard of Oz*.

On that early summer afternoon in Vancouver, Canada, resplendent in my royal blue and crimson ceremonial muumuu and deftly balancing the mortarboard yarmulke atop my bobbling head, I was given the opportunity to address assembled graduates and faculty, families and friends. Just as I had done on previous occasions, when similarly honored, I opened with a question: "What the hell were you people thinking? You are aware," I continued, "that I'm a high school dropout?"

Now that you have picked up this weighty tome from your local bookseller, I put the same question to you: *What the hell were you thinking?* Or, in the likelihood that someone else bought it for you as a graduation gift, you might want to ask them what the hell *they* were thinking. Not that I don't have some bona fides: I did receive my GED (General Equivalency Degree). I finally put in the effort to achieve this goal at the urging of my son. He was four at the time. I'd sit at the dining room table, Sam perched on my lap playing with a plastic dinosaur, while a math tutor schooled me in the finer points of the Pythagorean theorem. And so, at the tender age of thirty-two, with my son registered to begin kindergarten the next fall, I applied to take the test that would make me, for all intents and purposes, a high school graduate.

But that was 1994, approximately fifteen years after I left high school in the eleventh grade. In the intervening decade-and-a-half, I had been alternately fortunate and unfortunate enough to receive an amazingly comprehensive education, albeit unstructured, and often unbidden. Life 101.

Some lessons, of course, are more appropriate to a certain age or stage of development. For example, my latter teenage years into my early twenties was a time when I was just smart enough to get myself into situations I was still too stupid to get out of. Later, as evidenced by Sam's insistence that I finish what I started, I found out there is wisdom that can only come from being old enough to know how much there is to learn from children. And in the time since that milestone, I have remained a humble and grateful student of, if not the School of Hard Knocks, then at least the University of the Universal. I didn't pick my courses; they picked me. And just as there was no formal matriculation, neither was there any graduation. There were, of course, plenty of tests.

Just to reassure you, I'm not one of those swaggering jerks who, having achieved success after dropping out of school, promotes the fiction that a higher education is a complete waste of time. All the same, I sometimes employ my lack of academic standing as a subtle goad to those who would make character judgments based solely on one's alma mater or post-graduate degree.

As executive producer of *Spin City,* I was responsible for hiring and managing an astoundingly bright collection of young comedy writers, many of them graduates from prestigious universities: Dartmouth, Yale, Princeton, and Harvard, to name an ivy-covered few. Inspired by the irony that I was the boss of such a lettered group of individuals, and, honestly, perhaps a little intimidated, I thought I'd have some fun with it. I amassed a collection of T-shirts from some of the finest schools in the country. Among others, I had a burgundy Harvard tee and a Stanford Cardinal jersey. An old Dartmouth baseball shirt was a personal favorite. "Now," I announced to the wunderkinds, assembled for one of our first meetings of season one, "if you see me wearing a shirt from your alma mater, say Yale, for example" (with this I'd sneak a glance at an eager young Eli whose specialty was fart jokes), "then that means it's your day to get me coffee." Okay, so I am capable of a modicum of swaggering jerkitude.

A scant few minutes of Wikipedic surveying will uncover an impressive roster of well-known people, in every arena of public life, who have attained success and recognition without ever having graduated from high school. Those I most relate to are, of course, the actors and entertainers, whose early life experiences were no doubt similar to my own, propelled by a common group of neuroses toward careers in show business. These include such estimable personages as Leonardo DiCaprio, Johnny Depp, Robert De Niro, Chris Rock, Kevin Bacon, John Travolta, Hilary Swank, Jim Carrey, Charlie Sheen, Sean Connery, Al Pacino, and Quentin Tarantino.

But it's not just actors who have achieved success despite bailing on their formal education. Here's a group, sure to be a corkscrew to the gut of any CPA with an MBA, that includes some of the more impressive dropout *billionaires*: Richard Branson (founder of Virgin Music and Virgin Atlantic Airways); Andrew Carnegie (industrialist); Henry Ford (founder of the Ford Motor Company); John D.

Rockefeller (oilman); Philip Emeagwali (supercomputer scientist and one of the pioneers of the Internet); Kirk Kerkorian (investor and casino operator); and Jack Kent Cooke (media mogul and owner of the Washington Redskins).

And my favorite list: *geniuses* without diplomas, including Thomas Edison, Albert Einstein, and Benjamin Franklin.

To be fair, there isn't enough paper in the world to print a *Who's Who of Famous Persons Who Actually Finished High School.* And an argument can be made, I'm sure, that successful dropouts are even rarer in an increasingly competitive modern job market where degrees, diplomas, and technical knowledge carry more weight than ever. There are plenty of old-timers on these lists, for sure, but it more than makes the case that one can be smart without necessarily being "book smart." Just as the reverse is true. As Dan Quayle once held, "What a waste it is to lose one's mind. Or not to have a mind is being very wasteful. How true that is." Dan went to DePauw University and received his law degree from the University of Indiana. Oh, and he put in four years as the second most powerful man on the planet.

Still, there really is no substitute for a solid education to inform a maturing mind. The men and women on these lists may have prospered, not through avoidance of a classic education, but by finding a way, if not to replicate it, then to approximate it. Whether you go to school or set out on your own, certain lessons are unavoidable. Speaking from personal experience, it might be less painful to learn them in the classroom.

When Am I Ever Gonna Use This Stuff?

AS FOR MY OWN TRUNCATED SECONDARY EDUCATION, my head was in the clouds as my mom would say, or if you asked my father, up my ass.

In the outright creative subjects (drama, music, creative writing, other art electives, drawing, painting, and printmaking) I'd bring home A's. But any subject based on fixed rules, like math or chemistry or physics, sent my grades into free fall; the gold stars and smiley faces from grade school were long gone.

At report card time, I'd try to explain to my exasperated mother: "These are absolutes, Mom. They're boring. Take math, two plus two equals four. I mean, that's already on the books, right? Somebody's already nailed that down. What do they need me for? If someone's got a handle on how to get it to add up to five, count me in." Mom would sigh and hurry to sign the report card before Dad got home.

When red flags began to pop up on the school front, blue veins would pop up on Dad's forehead. A barely passing grade, or a call from school about a trip to the principal's office, prompted a harsh reprimand from Dad, followed by a probative grilling as to what the hell I was thinking and demands that I get my "ducks in a row forth-with." I wasn't failing out of rebellion though; I wasn't angry at my parents, or anybody else. Yet throughout junior high, my academic grades continued to plummet. The reprisals from Dad, once automatic, tapered off as he accepted their futility. He'd curl his lip, throw up his hands, and stalk off—that is, if I didn't slink off first.

By the time I entered high school, I had forsaken academics altogether in favor of my burgeoning acting career. An aptitude had become a passion and flowered into a dream. During much of the fall of 1978, I was going to school by day and performing at night in a long-running hit play at the Vancouver Arts Club, the big Equity theater company in town. I'd work at the theater until well after midnight every night, climb out of bed in the morning, go through the I'm-off-to-class motions, scramble into my pickup truck, proceed to the nearest park, pull under the cool shade of a maple tree, fish a foam pad out of the cab, slap it down in the bed of the truck, and go back to sleep.

My first class in the morning was drama, and I found myself in the strange position of receiving solid reviews for my professional acting at the same time I was flunking high school drama for too many absences. I pointed this irony out to my drama teacher, angling for credit for work experience. No soap. Truth is, her hands were tied by administrative policy.

Over time, it became clear that I was flunking just about every class I had. I gave notice that I would not be returning for classes in the spring. I made the rounds at school, cleaned out my locker, and said good-bye to friends and those teachers with whom I was still on speaking terms. Doubt about the wisdom of my decision was nearly unanimous. I remember one exchange, in particular, with a social studies teacher. "You're making a big mistake, Fox," he warned. "You're not going to be cute forever." I thought about this for a beat, shot him a smile, and replied, "Maybe just long enough, sir. Maybe just long enough."

My dad agreed to drive me down to Los Angeles to find an agent and begin to build a career. You might have expected him to protest, but having only stayed in school through eighth grade himself, he reasoned that although I was a screw-up in school, I was already making a decent wage as an actor. Of the move to California, he said, "Hey, if you're going to be a lumberjack, you'd better go to the forest."

Whoa, you the high school or college grad might be thinking right now. *That's a helluva lot different from my experience.* I don't know . . . is it? As I reflect on it now, it seems fairly representative of the rite of passage that millions of seventeen- and eighteen-year-olds go through every year. My leaving home was analogous to the experience of any fledgling college student. I gave myself four years to achieve my goal of becoming a steadily working actor, and what's more, I had a leg up on many of my peers heading off to State U. in that I already had my major, recognizing of course that it was not one offered by my erstwhile high school.

So my dad drove me to L.A. just like your parents likely drove you to Kenyon or Ball State, or whichever school of your choosing chose to have you. And the next four years provided as intense an undergraduate experience as one would expect from any college career, replete with parties and heavy workloads, not enough spare time, too much spare time, parties, deadlines, successes, failures, parties, heartaches, girlfriends, parties, ex-girlfriends, future girlfriends, parties, and a graduation of sorts. Was I nervous at first? Were you? Me neither, not really. I was pumped. I knew this was the next step for me, although one of the reasons it might have been so easy to make up my mind was that my brain, like the brain of any eighteen-year-old, was still under construction (trust me, I know from brains).

Teenagers blithely skip off to uncertain futures, while their parents sit weeping curbside in the Volvo, because the adolescent brain isn't yet formed enough to recognize and evaluate risk. That's why we can talk young men and women into fighting wars, and MTV and ESPN 2 are crowded with tattooed mohawk-wearers leaping buses on skateboards. The prefrontal cortex, sometimes known as the seat of reason, is the part of the brain that we use to make decisions. It's our bulwark against banzai behavior. A teenager's prefrontal cortex is still growing, still connecting up with other parts of the brain. It's the *amygdala,* home base for gut reactions and raw emotion, that's going full blast at this point. Not a lot of reasoned thinking going on there.

With so many immediate considerations to deal with, I don't know if my parents had time to ponder the broader implications of the odyssey I was embarking upon. As removed as they were from the world of showbiz, they might not have been informed enough to have specific fears, but they were still visited by worries that I could very well be sucked into a whirling vortex of depravity, exposed to a nonstop bacchanalia—a moveable feast of drunkenness, disorderly conduct, and brazen sexuality.

Sure, all that happened, but the party, it turned out, wasn't in Hollywood, but Westwood, the campus of UCLA. While I had no connection to the academic life at the university, I had become friends with three transfer students from the University of Maine, frat brothers who were living off campus while waiting for space to open up at the fraternity house. Temporarily occupying the apartment next to mine, the Maine-iacs (as I referred to them) were dealing with Orono-to-L.A. culture shock every bit as jarring for them as my own Canada-to-California adjustment. It was easy to recognize aspects of my own experience in theirs. Young, far from home, hoping to measure up to some still undefined standard, they studied their textbooks in pursuit of better grades, just as I pored over scripts in pursuit of better jobs.

Although we went our separate ways during work and school hours, my friends provided me with an entree into what were easily the best parts of life on campus—free beer and college girls. I remember thinking at the time that our situations were similar, but I allowed myself extra points for the pressure that came with trying to find the next job. "You've got it easy," I'd tell them. "Your parents bought you four more years of high school."

This was wrongheaded on a number of levels. For starters, college is a lot more demanding than high school—not that the demands of high school were all that familiar to me, given that I had made little effort to meet them. The other flaw in my pronouncement was that it made an easy assumption about who was footing the bill. My perception, rooted in my Canadian working-class background, was that behind each of these partying coeds were a beneficent and indulging American mom and pop, happily forking over cash to the university, who in turn would feed and water the kid for however long it took for the prefrontal cortex and amygdala to assume their proper weights in the balance of influence.

Floating my "four more years of high school" theory would provoke an earful in response. Did I have any idea what kinds of loans these guys were carrying? I had to admit, I didn't. Much of the expense of their formal education was front-loaded, whereas with my experiential education, I was, in effect, running a tab; especially dangerous, as I'll point out shortly, when you can't do basic math. So, we all felt the weight of expectation. Still, I felt more comfortable not to be carrying all that debt before I had even decided what was worth going into debt for.

Despite being an indifferent high school student, I always enjoyed reading, and was familiar with the story of Sisyphus. I pictured the Maine-iacs, with their student loans, as each having to push a large rock up a mountain. I began to understand that the rock was not the debt, but their course load. The debt was the mountain. Me, I was just dancing on the edge of a cliff.

So each of us, whether they off to college or me off to Hollywood, could be described as full of bluster and bravado, high expectations and low reservations. What separated us, perhaps, was that I lacked a blueprint.

As an exercise, I recently picked up a course catalogue from Hunter College, part of the City University of New York. Reading through the curriculum, I recognized how my life experiences could fit into a prescribed outline for an undergraduate education: the one I had supposedly missed out on. Laying out a series of typical college courses, as described in the catalogue, can help make a case that I have, to some extent, fulfilled the requirements for each particular course while having absolutely no idea I was doing it.

I might have skipped class, but I didn't miss any lessons.

PART II

Economics

Economics is the social science that deals with how best to use scarce resources to satisfy unlimited human needs and wants. Economics students become problem solvers. They learn to analyze a situation, figure out what is important, and determine what can be abstracted away.

IN A PURELY ACADEMIC SENSE, MOST OF WHAT I KNOW about economics I learned from Alex P. Keaton. My years of playing the archconservative, Milton Friedman–loving young capitalist gave me a passing familiarity with terms like "supply and demand," "gross national product," and "trickle-down economics." But with no personal fascination with the world of finance and market trends beyond my desire, as an actor, to be believable in the role, I often had to be careful not to hold the *Wall Street Journal* stock page upside down in front of the camera. Still, the years between my moving to the States and finally landing my role on *Family Ties* had provided me with an intense schooling in the basic laws of economics.

Fundamental concepts like "supply and demand" take on a whole new meaning when you, as an actor, are the "supply," and as hard as you might try, you find it impossible to drum up any "demand." And "trickle-down" was just another way of saying "You're pissing your money away before it even gets to you." Moreover, the mathematical absolutes I complained to my mother about earlier were now no longer just random numbers on a page, but specific bits of information relevant to my life, the mastery over which was crucial to my immediate survival. Simply put, I had to learn to meet the bottom line; *to analyze a situation, figure out what* was *important, and determine what* could *be abstracted away.*

The dimensions and amenities of my first Los Angeles apartment would strike the average dorm-dwelling college student as familiar: a seventeen-by-twelve-foot studio, with a microscopic bathroom—toilet, shower, no tub, and a bathroom sink. This was the apartment's only sink, and the basin was so tiny I'd have to take my dirty dishes with me into the shower. It wasn't uncommon for me to wash my hair with Palmolive and my dishes with Head & Shoulders. A closet doubled as the kitchen. But for $225 a month, with a six-month lease, I was in California, independent, and insanely happy.

An inventory of my worldly possessions as an eighteen-year-old on my own in Los Angeles: one duffel bag full of clothing (i.e., dirty laundry), one hot plate, some mismatched kitchenware, toiletries, blanket, bedsheets, and a wind-up alarm clock. Oh, and then there was the furniture: one mattress and one folding canvas director's chair.

I worked consistently at first, bit parts and guest spots in episodes of TV programs like *Family* and *Lou Grant,* and soon I landed a job as a regular on *Palmerstown, U.S.A.,* a CBS midseason pickup with an order for eight one-hour episodes. Then came more episodic TV work (*Trapper John, M.D., Here's Boomer*); a few commercials (McDonald's, Tilex Foaming Tub and Tile Cleaner); and a sort-of film, the schlock cinema classic *Class of 1984.* All in all, my first two-and-a-half years in Los Angeles had amounted to a reasonably successful run.

So why then, in less than three years, was I perilously near starvation? You could say that I was naïve, but then again, flat-out stupid would cover it. I had no patience for numbers and therefore no facility for keeping track of my debts and expenditures. I had not yet even begun to understand how to *best use scarce resources to satisfy unlimited human needs and wants.*

My agent, Bob, earned the standard 10 percent of my paycheck off the top, and for holding my hand, my managers, Sue and Bernie, took another 20 percent. Halfway through the first season of *Palmerstown,* my lease was up, and needing more space, I found a slightly larger but equally no-frills one-bedroom apartment in nearby Brentwood. The rent was almost double what I had been paying, $425, but in addition to a bathtub, this place boasted an actual kitchen sink.

There was a cupboard above the kitchen sink— ostensibly for dishes, it was where I kept my monster, those mathematical "absolutes" coming back to bite me on the ass. I developed a habit of collecting all my bills and threatening missives from creditors into a loose, disorganized bundle and jamming them into that cupboard above the kitchen sink: a growing paper monster. Not wanting to think about it, never mind actually look at it, I'd open the cupboard, feed it more red ink, then quickly slam the door shut. Out of sight, out of mind: a closet full of daunting, implacable absolutes.

I was earning SAG scale, the rock-bottom minimum rate, which barely covered the basics—apartment, clothing, car rental, food—plus business expenses (all those percentages). Then there was the government. I had overlooked a subtlety in my check stubs during that first year in L.A.: my employers hadn't been deducting state or federal taxes from my payments, and it never occurred to me that I should be putting any money aside for that purpose.

When I received my first tax bill from the IRS, I made a panicky call to my managers, and they recommended an accountant. This guy laid out an orderly method for applying present and future earnings toward paying off back taxes, for which services he would deduct from all present and future earnings 5 percent off the top. This brought my total up-front fees to a staggering 35 percent.

If I earned four thousand dollars in a month—which seemed like a lot of money in a teenager's wallet—I would picture the many things I could do with that four grand.

But by the time the check passed through the gauntlet of my financial obligations, I barely had enough left over for leftovers.

Regrettably, I hadn't spent enough time in math class to appreciate the power of those percentage deductions— and if I had ever sat down to actually do the math, it would've looked something like this:

$4,000	pay day
− 1,400	35% fees
− 1,200	taxes
− 425	rent
− 300	car payment, insurance, gas
− 100	utilities
− 150	audition clothes, headshots, publicity, etc.
− 450	food: allowance of only $15 a day
= (25)	

For those of you who haven't passed Econ 1 yet, the parentheses mean that I was twenty-five dollars in the hole at the end of the month. And that's without any extravagances like movie tickets or beer.

My CPA's blueprint for financial recovery never made it off the drawing board. Unable to work during a prolonged SAG strike in 1980, I was nearly broke going into the second and final season of *Palmerstown*. After the series was cancelled, there were a few jobs, but I barely earned enough to live on—and nowhere near enough to begin seriously paying down my debts. While most out-of-work actors can supplement their incomes by boxing groceries or waiting tables, my alien status made this impossible. The only way I could work legally in the U.S. was as an actor. I was in a bind.

Now and then, I'd receive a residual check for an old commercial or TV episode—usually small amounts that passed first through the hands of my agent and managers, taxes paid up front, so the figure I actually netted would be pitifully small. This is what they mean by "the life of the starving artist." Whether or not I was an artist at all was debatable, as I had no opportunity to develop my craft and no offers to do so. The starving part fit, though. My diet had been reduced to cans and boxes with declarative, generic labels like TUNA or MACARONI.

What few possessions I owned, like my furniture, I began to liquidate. Over a period of months, I sold off my sectional sofa, section by section. The buyer was another young actor living in my building. Adding insult to indigence was the incremental nature of the transaction, emphasizing, as it did, the inverse trajectories of our respective careers.

Given my situation, it might have been wise to pull the curtain. There would be no shame in returning to Canada and rethinking my options. But there was my debt to the IRS to consider. If I ran out on that, it'd be good-bye to the United States forever.

My telephone service had been cut off, so I had given my agent the number of the phone booth at a nearby Pioneer Chicken. I had taken to using it as my ersatz office. In the unlikely event that I received any offers, my agent could reach me there. Most often though, I used it to check in with him. But something began to happen. Without thinking about it in exactly these terms, I started to get my head around the idea of supply and demand. The business in which I was trying to succeed was one that offered huge reversals of fortune, if only you could convince someone to hire you. It all came down to this: make one last urgent push at commercial acceptance, or tread desperately in a sea of red ink.

So I worked harder than ever before on my auditions and paid more attention to my appearance. Most of my baby fat was gone by now, not through any dieting regimen, just good old-fashioned starvation. After casting calls, I'd use precious quarters to press my agent to follow up with casting directors. In short, I worked my ass off to earn the privilege of working my ass off . . . or at least working it out of debt. And it paid off. At the absolute fifty-ninth second of the fifty-ninth minute of the eleventh hour, I was cast as Alex Keaton on *Family Ties.* There I was, at the very same pay phone outside the chicken shack on San Vicente, negotiating my new contract.

Within months, I no longer had the problem of not having enough money. In my early twenties, in the L.A. of the early eighties, flush with the success of a hit television series, I now had a new problem (if you could call it that) . . . a raging amygdala and an American Express Gold Card.

Comparative Literature

Comparative literature courses are designed for students who are interested in a broad view of literature and in the diversity of literary cultures, literary movements, and genres.

MY LOVE OF READING ALMOST COST ME MY CAREER.

I had been in Los Angeles for six months and was halfway through the first season of *Palmerstown*. Returning to L.A. after a trip home for Christmas, I was detained by U.S. immigration agents, who inquired whether I was entering their country for work or pleasure. My employer had applied for the work permit that I, as a Canadian citizen, needed to work in the States, and though approved, the actual visa had not yet come through. Nervous about not having the document in hand, I asked the production staff what I should say to officials. "Keep it simple," they advised. "Don't go into a big song and dance about the paperwork. Tell them that you're just coming down to visit."

Those advising me didn't count on the tenacity of the men and women who guard the border. Nor could they have known that, while a fairly decent actor, I was a pathetic liar. And they soon found out that I was a total idiot. A tip to anyone who finds him- or herself in a similar predicament: INS won't believe you're going on vacation if (A) you're traveling on a one-way ticket; (B) you're carrying a suitcase full of dirty laundry; and (C) you are in possession of any scrap of evidence that you, in fact, reside in the foreign city you claim to be "just visiting." In my case, that scrap of evidence was my Beverly Hills library card.

One redeeming element of that story is that I had a library card. Being a starving actor, I couldn't afford to buy books, but I couldn't afford not to read books. If I were to peruse the library records of my reading preferences of that time, however, I'd probably cringe. I read mostly for entertainment, not edification, and if I happened upon a great piece of literature, it would have been through accident rather than intention. Even years later, when I bought my books instead of borrowing them, I was still a sucker for pulp fiction. A few months after we started dating, Tracy and I went on our first vacation together. On day one, each of us carried a book down to the beach. Tracy, I discovered, was reading *The Mayor of Casterbridge* by Thomas Hardy. I had Stephen King. I can't remember which of his books it was, but I do know it was one of the heavier ones (two or three pounds at least).

In terms of "comparative" literature, one might ask, "What are we comparing it to?" Me, personally, I most often compare books to their film adaptations. It's an interesting exercise. Here's a quick list of five that come to mind, as well as my own humble assessment as to whether the material was best served by the author or the filmmaker. Simply put, which was better, the book or the movie?

1. THE GODFATHER Francis Ford Coppola, 1972
Based on the book by Mario Puzo, 1969

While Mario Puzo's florid pulp epic, rendered with verve and velocity, is the kind of thing I might busy myself with on vacation while Tracy rereads *The Agony and the Ecstasy*, it doesn't measure up to the Francis Ford Coppola masterpiece it inspired. Characters that are clichéd on the page mesmerize on the screen thanks to the artistry of Brando, Pacino, Duvall, and Cazale.

2. JAWS Steven Spielberg, 1975
Based on the book by Peter Benchley, 1974

The novel was a page-turner, but Steven Spielberg's breakthrough film was a stomach-turner (and I mean that in a good way). It's one thing to read about a Great White devouring Captain Quint. It's a whole different kettle of fish to watch the thing munch on Robert Shaw. In fairness to Peter Benchley, I also prefer John Huston's retelling of *Moby Dick* over Melville's novel.

3. MOBY DICK John Huston, 1956
Based on the book by Herman Melville, 1851

Seriously, go back and read the thing . . . it takes forever just to get on the boat.

4. FIGHT CLUB David Fincher, 1999
Based on the book by Chuck Palahniuk, 1996

The first rule of Fight Club: You do not talk about Fight Club. I will say this, though. Great book. Great movie. Technical draw.

5. 2001: A SPACE ODYSSEY Stanley Kubrick, 1968
Book by Arthur C. Clarke, 1968

This is a tricky one. Clarke's book was actually published after the release of Kubrick's film, and each man worked on his version concurrent with the other. Visually, the film was stunning and the atmospherics were sensational. But I have to admit, only after reading Clarke's book was I able to discern a plot. Edge to Arthur C. Clarke. Interesting note: just recently, I learned from my son, Sam, that "HAL," the name given to the film's mutinous computer, is a play on a familiar acronym. "H-A-L" are the three letters that precede IBM in the alphabet.

. . .

WHILE THIS IS fun to do, the list of page-to-screen adaptations is a long one, and you probably have your own favorites. When comparing the positive and negative qualities of books and movies, keep in mind the storytelling advantages of each medium. The novelist has the benefit of exposition, interior dialogue, and imagination unlimited by production costs. And the director can employ dynamic visuals and harness the visceral power of the actors' performances.

I know firsthand the difficulties inherent in turning a popular book into a successful movie—witness *Bright Lights, Big City*.

On second thought . . . read the book.

Physics

Physics is the study of the basic interactions that govern the behavior of the universe as we know it. As such, a knowledge of physics is necessary for the proper understanding of any science.

WHAT I APPRECIATE MOST ABOUT THE LAWS OF PHYSics is their indifference to my feelings about them. Compliance is not optional. Their absolutism is much more tangible than strict mathematics, where proof requires countless squiggles on a blackboard. A lesson in physics can be as simple as standing under a falling brick . . . or pissing in the wind . . . or attempting to stuff ten pounds of shit into a five-pound bag.

There were plenty of times, when I was young, that I would unwittingly test the limits of these governing laws of universal behavior. And there were other times when I would confirm their authority without even being aware that I was doing so. Take, for example, my days as an undersized youth hockey player; game after game, I'd throw my sixty-pound frame in the path of much bigger players, only to dissolve into a pile of goo on the ice surface. Eventually, I discovered that setting myself correctly in the path of an onrushing opponent and angling my shoulder at the precise midpoint of his jersey would flip that bad boy right onto his ass. I didn't understand that I was harnessing the power of physics. I had no concept of fulcrums, weight transference, centers of gravity, or actions having equal and opposite reactions. I broke it down this way: The bigger they are, the harder they fall.

In time, my appreciation for physics became more nuanced. "The only reason for time is so that everything doesn't happen at once." As a teenager, I didn't know to attribute the above quote to everyone's favorite long-haired genius, Albert Einstein. I picked it up from someone else and passed it off as my own, usually as a lame explanation for my tardiness for school, or dinner, or whatever. I thought it was funny. My father, an army lifer who kept a precise, military clock, wasn't as amused (although he might have been impressed if either of us knew I was quoting Einstein). Einstein, of course, had a lot to say about the laws of physics as they concern all matters temporal, theorizing at one point that ". . . the distinction between past, present, and future is only a stubbornly persistent illusion." This may be the only context in which Albert and I might be mentioned in the same sentence: time travel. Like it says on the movie poster: "He was never in time for his classes . . . He wasn't in time for dinner . . . Then one day . . . he wasn't in his time at all."

For many people, Marty McFly embodies a possibility about which the world's greatest physicists have only hinted. I am constantly bombarded with questions regarding the space-time continuum, string theory, and flux capacitors. Believe me, I am not being coy when I respond with complete and utter ignorance: *It was a movie, folks. And, by the way, there's no such thing as a hoverboard either* (more about that later). I will say this, though. *Back to the Future* did provide me with an opportunity to, if not defy the limits set forth by the laws of physics, then to stretch them well beyond what I would ever have thought possible. There were many times during our whirlwind shooting schedule when the lines of reality began to blur, and I could have sworn I was actually in two places at once.

I took on the role of Marty McFly in January of 1985. Director Bob Zemeckis and his crew had already been shooting with another actor for five weeks when they decided a change was necessary. Steven Spielberg, the film's executive producer, approached his good friend, *Family Ties* creator Gary David Goldberg, and inquired about my availability to take over the role. This wasn't the first time Steven had considered me to play Marty. Before production on *Back to the Future* even began, he had approached Gary about my availability. But with a whole season of shooting ahead, Gary reluctantly concluded that it would be impossible to release me. I knew nothing of the request.

Now, months later, with only half a season of *Ties* remaining, my TV boss allowed that it might be possible and called me into his office to tell me about the offer. I jumped at the opportunity. Although Gary was happy for me, he did offer this gentle warning: "You realize you're not going to miss an hour of work on the show. You'll be here every day and in every scene as usual. The movie you can shoot at nights and on weekends, or whenever you're not here. It's up to you."

Young, ambitious, and convinced of my own invincibility, I laughed in the face of eighteen- and twenty-hour work days, undaunted at the prospect of shuttling from Paramount Studios to Universal Studios to location, and back to Paramount again.

Cut to three weeks in, and I had been reduced to a state of functioning dementia. As promised, I would go in and rehearse *Family Ties* all day, be picked up by a teamster with a bag of fast food (or maybe just a milkshake) to be consumed during the twenty-minute drive through Cahuenga Pass to the film studio, where I'd work until 2:00 or 3:00 A.M., at which point the same teamster would drive me to my apartment and, sometimes literally, carry me into bed. Four or five hours later that same morning, a different driver (the union protected them from submitting to the same schedule I was on) would come into my apartment, turn on the shower, arouse me from my coma, and deliver me back to the TV show.

Studies have shown that intense sleep deprivation can have disastrous effects on the body, trigger hallucinations, and in extreme cases, cause temporary insanity. I experienced confusion as to what set I was on at any given time, which characters I was interacting with, what wardrobe

I was wearing, and basically who I was in the first place. More than once, I referred to Steven Keaton as Doc Brown and panicked before entering the kitchen set on show night when I realized I wasn't wearing my orange, down-filled vest. The filming schedule redefined for me what is possible and impossible. Luckily, for roughly two hours or so, *Back to the Future* did the same thing for moviegoers.

No matter how fantastic a movie's premise is, there are always a special few who buy in and accept the craziest shit at face value, like the hoverboard. I've fielded more questions about hoverboards than any other aspect of the trilogy. Otherwise sane people were convinced that these devices actually existed, especially after Bob Zemeckis made tongue-in-cheek comments to the press about parent groups preventing toy manufacturers from putting them on the market (this resulted in hundreds of kids calling Mattel, demanding hoverboards for Christmas). Believe me, if someone had actually devised and manufactured a flying skateboard capable of propelling a surfer on an invisible wave of air, he didn't let me in on the secret. It could have spared me from hours of dangling like a flesh-and-blood Pinocchio. Alternately strapped into every manner of harness, hinged leg brace,

and flying apparatus the most sadistic special-effects en-
gineers could devise, my foot stapled to that pink piece of
plastic, I spent hours attached to metal cables, swinging
from sixty-foot cranes, back and forth across the Court-
house Square set.

During the filming of this sequence, Tracy was preg-
nant with our son, Sam. I carried a beeper at all times (this
was pre-cell phone), for the sole purpose of alerting me in
the event of incipient labor (or in the lexicon of physics, the
fetus reaching critical mass). Thank God it never beeped
when I was "hoverboarding" because there wouldn't have
been a damn thing I could have done about it.

When describing me, Tracy often refers to a well-known
concept of physics: "inertia." As Newton avers in his first
law: *An object that is not moving will not move until a force
acts upon it. An object that is moving will not change its
velocity until a net force acts upon it.* In other words, de-
pending on what's happening in my life at any given moment, I can either be the laziest human being on the
planet, or the busiest. I'm perfectly content to do absolutely
nothing until I'm catalyzed by some person or project, and
then I go nonstop until some countervailing force acts upon
me, and I revert back to static mode.

Now that I think of it, Newton could just as easily have had Parkinson's disease in mind. It has me in constant motion until such time as we can (and will) discover a force to arrest its velocity. In a metaphysical sense, though, I've often made the argument that PD itself was the force that arrested the sometimes aimless expenditure of kinetic energy I engaged in as a younger man. My formula: I couldn't be still until I could no longer be still.

Even a high school dropout is smart enough to know that he can't break Newton's first law. But maybe I found a way to tweak it a bit.

Political Science

Political Science deals with the various political, social, and cultural arrangements through which people govern their lives.

MY INTEREST IN POLITICS DATES BACK TO JUNIOR HIGH, when I was a volunteer vote-counter for the Liberal Party of British Columbia (turned out I didn't have to count that high). Whether through osmosis, intellectual curiosity, or a sense of civic responsibility, my son, Sam, now in college, has developed his own fascination with the political process. Like many people his age, Sam was energized by the last presidential election and got involved in the campaign. So it made sense for the two of us to be exactly where we were on the morning of January 20, 2009: freezing our asses off on the National Mall in Washington, D.C., while Barack Hussein Obama took the oath of office as the forty-fourth president of the United States. Broader politics aside, the occasion had particular importance for me, as the incoming president had promised to overturn Bush-era restrictions on stem cell research, against which I had campaigned so vigorously during the '06 midterm election.

According to polling, most Americans favor federally funded stem cell research, so from a political perspective, why did we have to fight so hard for it to go forward? The answer is both basic and complex. George Bush's policy itself wasn't on the ballot; the voter had to discern for him- or herself how a given candidate felt about the research restrictions and whether or not they would vote to overturn them. As citizens, we all have beliefs, ethical concerns, fears, wants, and needs, in an order of importance known only to us. So the candidate and his pollsters endeavor to calculate which issues, as part of the larger matrix, we are willing to abandon or put aside. If you're liberal to moderate, you probably favor stem cell research, and on your list of the ten issues most important to you, put it at eight. If you're conservative and anti–stem cell research, you may have it in your top three. In the spirit of divide and conquer, a canny, uncommitted pol, with no strong personal commitment to one side or the other, realizes that the issue is more of a hot button for the conservative side, and pushes it to win the right.

I wanted to remind people that we were not dealing in the abstract. This issue affects them as well as one hundred million other Americans, for whom it rises to the level of life or death. One thing I absolutely was not saying is that those on the other side of the issue have any less compassion, empathy, or concern for the sick and suffering. Many who oppose embryonic stem cell research feel just as strongly that theirs is a truly compassionate position.

Politicians, however, by exploiting medical research as a "wedge issue," held the future hostage. So it was heartening to engage so many Americans in a conversation and empower them to make an informed decision, one way or the other. As it turned out, fifteen out of seventeen of the pro–stem cell candidates that I campaigned for in 2006 won their races. And just maybe, Obama's position on this research was at least a small factor in his 2008 presidential win.

TV talking heads proclaim every election cycle that pollster data predict apathy among college-age voters.

Young voters have heard over and over again that the "youth vote" will not turn out. As with wedge issues, this is yet another method employed to discourage participation in the political process by those who may disrupt the status quo—convincing them that their vote is meaningless.

It wasn't until late in the 2008 contest that pundits realized polling firms calling landlines weren't reaching young people—who for the most part used only cell phones.

It all comes down to the individual: to you. What do you want? Those who would try to convince you that your vote won't make a difference are right only if you don't exercise it. Don't just weigh in on the big stuff—presidential, congressional, and gubernatorial elections. Show up at the local level too: mayor, city council, dog catcher. Democracy is a big muscle. Flex it and put it to work.

I've lived in the States for thirty years now, but it was only a decade ago that I became a U.S. citizen. As a father, I needed to have a say in shaping the country my children were born in. By giving each of us a vote, our country holds out the opportunity, as well as the responsibility, to create the future we deserve.

Geography

Courses include human geography, physical geography, earth systems science, environmental studies, and geology. Students develop an awareness of earth phenomena and the role these play in people's lives.

"WHEREVER YOU GO, THERE YOU ARE."

My father used to say that all the time, and I easily dismissed it as Dadspeak, something I was meant to nod at in apparent agreement, so as not to provoke him to expound upon it further. Years later, it made a great deal of sense to me. However, I have now added a slight variation to that aphorism: "Wherever you go, there *it is*." The succinct summation of both of these thoughts is that wherever you travel, you have to adapt to your new surroundings. They won't adapt to you.

Back in 1987, shooting the Vietnam drama *Casualties of War* with Sean Penn and director Brian DePalma, I had the privilege of witnessing how a particular part of the planet—in this case the Southeast Asian island of Phuket, Thailand—resisted the attempts of a big budget Hollywood crew to transform it into anything other than what nature, climate, geology, botany, and biology intended it to be. In fact, all the crew was trying to do was make the place into another version of itself. Let me explain.

We had a series of nighttime jungle-combat scenes to film. Understandably, the difficulty of running camera-dolly tracks through the rain forest, along with a plethora of other practical issues, made it impossible for our crew to work in the actual jungle. So, Brian and his technicians went to plan B. The idea was to approximate a jungle in a large barren area that once was wooded, but had long since been dedicated to some kind of gravel mining—a quarry of sorts. They picked a parcel of land on the edge of a series of cliffs. Into these cliffs they had dug a network of tunnels, or half tunnels, exposed to Brian's cameras. The bonus was that Brian could get frighteningly atmospheric shots of Viet Cong crawling, weapons ready, through the tunnels beneath the jungle floor, then pan up slowly to find American

GIs patrolling unawares. To create this illusion, set decorators brought in hundreds of potted trees and plants and dug a small pond, all covering approximately an acre or so. Shortly after the new greenscape was in place, Brian and cast were able to rehearse scenes to be shot a few weeks later.

What happened next provided a lesson in "wherever you go, there it is." The surrounding flora and fauna quickly responded to our changes to the environment by reclaiming it. They subsumed it, overtook it. As if it were nothing more than a giant petri dish, the seasonal rains and sweltering humidity acted upon the "set," fomenting a riot of uncontained growth. Birds filled the canopy. Snakes moved in after them. Plants that only a few weeks before had been mere vestigial shoots poking their way through the forest floor now grew tendrils several meters long, which crept atop the soil to assert death grips around newly transplanted palm trees, entangling the feet of clumsy actors who had rehearsed in the exact same place only a few days before. Night scenes necessitated large, carbon-powered arc lamps and other Hollywood lighting equipment. This attracted swarms of insects, whose size, shape, and violent dispositions were so unearthly that only the most dedicated entomologist would have dared to capture them for identification.

At one point, I remember struggling to absorb a piece of acting direction from Brian, a large and imposing man of concentrated seriousness. He seemed bothered by my distraction as he laid out his interpretation of my character's present dilemma. "I'm sorry, Brian," I apologized. "I'm paying attention. It's just that there's a Volkswagen crawling up your arm." At that, the unflappable DePalma flapped, waving his arms to shake loose the scarab-like creature. I'm still half-surprised that it didn't carry him away. The new sets served the filmmaker's purposes, and I'm sure conditions were far better than they would have been in a pre-existing jungle, but the rapidity and enthusiasm with which the surrounding ecosystem replicated itself on this formerly barren patch of Thailand was a humbling reminder of the power of nature and the purity of place. *Wherever you go, there it is.*

Just as you can't change the essential nature of a place, don't count on the place to change the essential nature of you. It may be tempting, at some point in life, to seek a fresh start or even establish a new identity by uprooting from one location and transplanting physically to another. This is what pop psychologists and people in recovery refer to as "doing a geographic."

But for young people, who are defined by a sense of rootlessness, new places and new experiences can be savored for their own sake. In my early twenties, my hope was not that travel be transformative, but simply that it be fun. The first time I ventured to Mexico, for example, did not involve the exploration of Mayan ruins or the study of the people and their culture. My most striking memory was falling shirtless over a cliff in Cabo. As I tumbled through the cactus and over the rocky outcroppings, I struggled for control. I wasn't worried about being injured. I was worried about spilling my beer. I landed with a thud at the bottom of a small arroyo. Exhilarated that I still had a full bottle of Tecate, I was at first unaware of the six-inch slash on my right shoulder. Typical ignorant gringo that I was, I wanted no part of the local hospital, trusting instead the advice of the crew on our chartered fishing boat the next day, who advised me to douse the wound in tequila and let it cauterize in the Mexican sun. See, I might not have gone to college, but I didn't miss Spring Break. That's not travel, though, that's an incursion.

From childhood road trips across Canada in the family Pontiac to my most recent adventures in Bhutan, high in the Himalayas (more about this later), travel has always been a big part of my life. Even when my trips are predicated on business and not pleasure, on location shoots like that one in Thailand, or publicity junkets in Europe and Asia to promote new movies and television projects, I always take the time to appreciate where I am for what it is. I seek out the excitement of the strange and not the comfort of the familiar. I'm not trying to lose myself, or even find myself, for that matter. My goal is just to enjoy myself, learn something, and gain an appreciation for the amazing complexity of this planet and the people who live on it.

Wherever I go, I bring myself. And so far, it's always been a roundtrip.

PART III

Pay Attention Kid,
You Might Learn Something

FOR ALL THE HELP I'VE HAD ALONG THE WAY, I AM still prone to the delusion that I figured it all out myself. I used to tell people that I was an autodidact, then smile smugly when I could tell, by the look on their face, that I was so autodidactic that I had taught myself a word they didn't even know. *What a schmuck.* I do understand that the greatest influences in my life have been and remain those folks who keep me connected to the world around me and concerned with the people in it.

John Wooden, venerated coach of the UCLA men's basketball team during its dynasty years, recently celebrated his ninety-ninth birthday. To mark the occasion, ESPN interviewed Bill Walton, the gangly, garrulous center on two of Wooden's ten championship teams. Not really an interview, it was more of a *soliloquy*, with Walton launching into stanza after stanza of breathless praise for a man who had obviously influenced him in a profound and formative way. The stories and remembrances were peppered with Woodenisms that Walton and his fellow Bruins probably heard every day on the court during their college careers. "If you don't have time to do it right, when will you have time to do it over?" As well as: "It isn't what you do, but how you do it." And my personal favorite: "Things turn out best for the people who make the best of the way things turn out."

But it was obvious that the coach's relationship with these young men transcended basketball. More than a coach, to Bill Walton at least, John Wooden had become a mentor. And it must have been a complicated relationship; in Walton's voice, it was easy to hear not only his obvious affection and regard for his maestro, but also an ache as well, an enigmatic sense of remorse and regret, vestiges of a situation, or situations, when the bond had been threatened. After all, the formative years of their relationship coincided with the escalation in Vietnam, and Walton's youthful rebellion must have been an uneasy mix, at times, with Wooden's old-school conservatism. Perhaps it would have been easier for Wooden to remain purely the coach: to motivate, organize, maybe even inspire, but not risk seeing his players as any more than the means to another winning season.

Bill Walton's tribute brought to mind the gratitude I feel toward a number of people in my own life who have taken the time to express a belief in me, teach me, encourage me, inspire me, or just steer my ass out of oncoming traffic. And there have been a few whose shepherding of me toward my better interests surely qualifies them as mentors.

Ross Jones, my junior high drama teacher, awakened in me an understanding that a creative life could, indeed, be a productive life, and that it was perfectly acceptable to consider a career in acting. He was that rare authority figure who didn't mind stirring things up a bit. When I think of Ross, I think of two words that he would say again and again. A sly grin would appear on his thin, bearded face, framed by a mop of hair radically long for a teacher, even in the seventies. He'd splay his hands out in front of him like a close-up magician revealing his palms and ask, rhetorically, "Why not?"—a textbook piece of mentoring. Mr. Jones awakened in me a penchant for questioning and an acceptance of possibility as infinite.

Teachers and coaches, with exceptions like Ross and Coach Wooden, are distinct from mentors in that they have broader agendas, to adhere to the lesson plan or focus on the interests of the team, not the individual. They may develop a special interest in you, but they don't choose you, nor you them. In the same way, I don't include parents in my own definition of mentors, although parents are undoubtedly the principal influence in most of our lives. They brought us into the world and they may do everything in their power to get us through it safely, but in a way, that's their job.

On the subject of family, I do credit my mother's mother, Nana, for the space I was given as a child to be a dreamer and to color outside the lines. I was so irrepressibly quirky and impossibly tiny for the first ten years or so of my life, most of the adults around me were dubious that I could ever become a fully functioning adult member of society: "What's he going to do when he grows up—if he grows up?"

"Don't worry about him," Nana would assure them. "Michael will do more in his life than you can ever imagine." Her pronouncement carried the considerable weight of her reputation in the family as a proven psychic (among other premonitions, during the Second World War, after two of her sons were missing in action and presumed dead, she foretold the exact circumstances of their safe return, the details of which came to her in a dream). Believe it or not, the accuracy of her past predictions secured a great deal of wiggle room for me. Nana died when I was ten, but she had already bequeathed to me the benefit of the doubt when it came to opinions about my prospects. Nana's unflagging belief in her grandson had a profound effect on the path I chose and the willingness of others to grant me safe passage.

If not a mentor, then a role model, my brother, Steve, provided an example to be followed. Steve is a solid guy—playing by the rules and enjoying the hell out of life while doing it. In fact, his solidity probably made it easier for me to be a flake: *Well, Mike may be a washout, but at least Steve will be all right.* My big brother, mensch that he is, never used that as a club against me. Eight years his junior, I always felt (and still do) that Steve likes me. And while I make choices that he might find unconventional and shy away from, he supports me. Always a few years ahead of me in the milestone department, marriage, kids, etc., Steve laid out a primer for how to do things right. He and his wife are devoted to each other. They have a daughter and two sons, the eldest born with special needs. He greeted each challenge with grit, smarts, and compassion. He stepped up for Mom and the rest of us in a big way when our dad passed away. To this day, Steve is the only guy with whom I can spend more than thirty seconds on the telephone. In fact, sometimes our calls stretch on for hours. He's unaware that he's mentoring me—we're just shooting the shit.

Outside of family, the most significant mentor figure in my life has undoubtedly been Gary David Goldberg who, in his role as creator and executive producer of *Family Ties*, rescued me from poverty, plucked me from obscurity, and, in many ways, helped to prepare me for challenges and opportunities I never saw coming. Gary was Mr. Miyagi to my Karate Kid, Crash Davis to my "Nuke" LaLoosh, Doc Brown to my Marty McFly . . . well, no . . . I guess Christopher Lloyd was Doc to my Marty, but then, Gary had a hand in that too.

Gary didn't even want to hire me at first. For the role of Alex Keaton in *Family Ties*, Gary had Matthew Broderick in mind. When Matthew passed on the role and Gary started to audition other actors, I was the very first of hundreds to read for Alex. Judith Weiner, the casting director, loved my audition. Gary hated it. Weeks went by, and at the end of every fruitless casting session, Judith would get in Gary's ear and suggest that he give me another shot. Finally, Gary relented and in I went again, broke, starving, and incredibly motivated. Within a matter of minutes, Gary had gone from seeing me only to humor Judith, to being my number one fan.

Having won Gary over didn't completely secure my employment. He then had to sell me to a less than enthusiastic NBC, which had serious questions about my prospects as a TV star. "I don't know, Gary," said network chief Brandon Tartikoff. "I just can't see this kid's face on a lunchbox." Nonplussed and impatient with the lunchbox criteria, Gary, the indomitable battler, fought for me when it would have been just as easy to appease the higher-ups and move on. The realization that Gary believed in me validated this crazy gambit I had undertaken. I wouldn't have presumed that this bushy-bearded, bear-like comedy writer/producer would ever become my mentor, but vaguely aware of the stand he was taking on my behalf, I understood that I at least had a champion. All I ever wanted was a chance. Now someone was giving me a shot and, in the process, putting one of his own bullets at stake.

"All I know is I write him two jokes, he gets me three laughs" is how Gary put it to the network upon completion of the *Family Ties* pilot. The live taping had gone well, audience reaction had been enthusiastic, and they responded strongly to the Alex character. Like any protégé, I wanted to make my benefactor look like a genius. Well, he might already have been a genius, but at least I didn't prove him a fool. A common showbiz term, Komedy Kollege (yes, with two "K"s) was perhaps the only post-secondary education I was qualified for. I majored in the double take. Gary had a distinct understanding of comedy, and through his skills as a producer and talents as a writer, he transformed a kid who had never done comedy before into a young actor who had the chops and poise to carry a network TV show.

I committed my fair share of screw-ups over the next few years and admittedly came close to careening off the rails more than once during the eighties, but I'm convinced that without Gary looking out for me, my relatively sudden success would have been even more perilous. Show up to work on time, learn my lines, respect the writers, strive with every performance, every scene, every line, to improve on what I had done before: these were the standards that Gary expected me to meet. It was an ethic I understood. It was basically my father's. I locked it in, and try to honor it still.

Our backgrounds, though completely different on the surface, were, viewed more closely, made up of the same stuff. Sure, Gary was a product of forties and fifties Brooklyn, and I came of age on various military bases across Canada during the sixties and seventies. But both of us were raised by close families of modest means, and each of us proved to be the wild card in our respective familial decks.

Following each Friday night taping at the height of *Family Ties'* success, the cast, crew, and writers would head to an elegant but welcoming French restaurant a block or two away from Paramount Studios on Melrose in Hollywood to eat, drink, and party. Usually the last to leave, Gary and I would linger at the table, polishing off the dregs of whatever indecently expensive Cabernet we had ordered, and *kvell*. Gary would launch into the story of how he came to be sitting at that victory table, tracing his journey from playing stickball on the streets of Brooklyn, to basketball at Brandeis, to dropping out of college, to Greece, where he lived in a cave with his future bride, Diana, and their well-traveled Labrador, Ubu, to the birth of their daughter, to surviving on food stamps, to a spec script, to a career. A story he never tired of telling and I never tired of hearing, it was every bit as improbable as my own. "Mike," he would say, clapping a meaty, fur-coated hand on my bony, freckled forearm with unintended force, "you know what we did? We jumped worlds. This wasn't supposed to happen to us. We are the luckiest guys on the planet." To this day, the word that comes to mind when I think of Gary is "gratitude." None of us is entitled to anything. We get what we get, not because we want it or we deserve it or because it's unfair if we don't get it, but because we earn it, we respect it, and only if we share it do we keep it.

As I said earlier, Gary made a second huge bet on me, one that many of his advisors counseled him against. Just as *Family Ties* was hitting its stride, he allowed me, after an initial hesitation, to do *Back to the Future*. As I was contractually tied to the show, there was no obligation or expectation that Gary should take a risk that I might find success on the big screen and finagle my way out of the TV series. I rewarded his faith with complete loyalty, and though I found worldwide success as Marty McFly, I re-doubled my commitment to Alex P. Keaton.

Tougher days lay ahead. Our mentor/mentee relationship would be tested, just as Bill Walton's and Coach Wooden's had (as I had inferred from watching Walton's interview on ESPN). Seven years after Gary and I had mutually agreed to end *Family Ties* while it was still on top, we re-teamed for the ABC series *Spin City*. We were thrilled about working together again, but I felt some trepidation. Before renewing our professional relationship, I explained to Gary that we had to make some adjustments to our respective roles that reflected a number of wholesale shifts that had occurred in my life during the intervening years. I was now married with three children, had been diagnosed with PD, had quit drinking, and had moved to New York City, where I insisted the new show be filmed. Gary offered no objection to producing the show in New York rather than his home base in L.A. It was also very important to me that we be equal partners going forward.

The show, when it hit the air, was a big success, both creatively and commercially. But by the second season, tensions were mounting. It's not that this new dynamic was so wrong; it was that the old one was so right. Gary decided to bow out. We had a kind of half-assed standoff for a few months, maybe a year, but our affection and respect for each other absorbed the strain and negated it. When the advance of my illness necessitated my early retirement, Gary returned for my last few episodes of the show, and our friendship grew stronger than ever. I'm convinced it was our gratitude that saved us. *The rocks— not the sand. Hold the beer, but pour Gary some wine.*

We will always be those two guys in the restaurant, leaning back in upholstered French armchairs before the vestiges of a banquet, sipping on our wine and exclaiming, "Can you friggin' believe this?"

A few days ago, Gary dropped by my office in New York. We walked down the block to Madison Avenue for coffee at this little neighborhood café, a place where local private school moms stop in for lattes after drop-off. No longer two Young Turks on the rise, commandeering a pricey bistro until the wee hours, we now sat at this modest table, two contented middle-aged men, each on either end of their fifties, still marveling at their ridiculously good fortune. I was pleased to see Gary looking so trim and healthy, and was particularly moved by the look of contentment that washed over his face as he described the life that he and his longtime love, Diana, were now leading at their home in rural Vermont. Explaining how the two of them, up there in the Green Mountains, had managed to dial down life's urgencies and dial up its pleasures and richness, Gary put it beautifully and poetically: "We've discovered a way," he confided with a sense of gleeful wonderment, *"to bend time."* I imagined Tracy and me engaged in a similar conspiracy a dozen years or so from now. It was a nice feeling. I realized, in that moment, that I still have a lot to learn from Gary—that he'd always be my mentor. He may not be ninety-nine yet, but that's my soliloquy.

If you're lucky, at some point in the future when you're in need of guidance, or maybe just moral support, you will cross paths with a suitable mentor. Even luckier, you'll realize you've had one in your life all along, and you'll gain a new appreciation for how you benefited from that relationship. The luckiest circumstance of all, of course, is a combination of the two. You've had help all along, and as the path widens or narrows, whatever the case may be, new and powerful influences will enter your life and aid your progress.

In my experience, a mentor doesn't necessarily tell you what to do, but more importantly, tells you what *they* did or might do, then trusts you to draw your own conclusions and act accordingly. If you succeed, they'll take one step back, and if you screw up, they'll take one step closer. Whatever it is they teach you . . . pass it on.

PART IV

Victims of Pomp
and Circumstance

"It's what you learn after
you know it all that counts."

JOHN WOODEN

HERE YOU ARE, YOU'VE PULLED IT OFF . . . AFTER
years of jumping through hoops, meeting, sometimes
surpassing, expectations, you've made it. You've broken
through to the light, even though it often seemed there was
only night at the end of the tunnel. Congratulations on your
achievement.

Going forward, if you put in the work, you'll reap the
reward, just like in school. You will probably find useful
and marketable applications for the skills you've developed. Many of the friends you've made over the last few

years will stay with you, and along with your family and the new friends you meet along the way, they will form a network of support and contacts that will open new doors and keep you safe behind old ones. You'll be emboldened to challenge yourself and to embark on unexpected journeys. Maybe you'll fall in love or remain committed to a school sweetheart. There might be kids, a dog, a yard—if that model fits your ideal. Perhaps you have a less conventional lifestyle in mind, custom designed by and for you. Life is good, and there's no reason to think it won't be—right up until the moment when everything explodes into a fireball of tiny, unrecognizable fragments, or it all goes skidding sideways, through the guardrail, over the embankment, and down the mountain. This will happen (and probably more than once).

What I've just described may be shocking coming from me, given my reputation as an optimist. Although I like the identification, it's not exactly the way I would characterize my outlook. I think I am a realist. The reality is that things change; the question is, how will I perceive that change, and am I willing to change along with it?

It may seem hard to believe, but it's catastrophe that offers the most promise for an even richer life. This is the gateway to the good stuff. In other words, you never truly know which way the wind is blowing until the shit hits the fan. And further, if you don't mind getting a little dirty, that breeze will carry you a long way.

I'm assuming that you have, up to this point, accepted my premise that we all pass through an education of sorts. Mine, although perhaps not as structured as yours, was composed of the same fundamental lessons, leading to a point of readiness to take steps without so much guidance from other parties, save select mentors. In other words, I've learned enough to be safely unleashed on society. In surviving those first few years in Hollywood and the first few years of my initial success, I passed through a crucible of sorts and forged a life that many would view as exemplary of the American Dream.

On the career front, I had captured lightning in a bottle more than once. On television with *Family Ties* and in film with *Back to the Future*, as well as with other projects, I had arrived at a place far beyond the simple working actor status that I sought when I left Canada for Los Angeles as a teenager. I met a girl too smart and too beautiful for me by a long shot, and I somehow persuaded Tracy to marry me. We soon had a healthy son. We lived in luxurious homes, drove foreign cars, and traveled to faraway, exotic places. In short, life just couldn't get any better. But it would, though only after it got much worse.

In 1990, when Sam was six months old, my father died unexpectedly. Suddenly a father to a son, but no longer a son to a father, I finally began to understand the value of my dad's experience and advice only when it was lost to me. Later, after a number of body blows left me sucking for air, I would realize that my dad continues to be a guiding force years after his passing. It's ironic, given his "prepare for the worst" philosophy and my happy appetite for risk, that his death should be the harbinger of the toughest period of my life: graduate school for the soul.

Within a year, I started to exhibit symptoms of Parkinson's disease: twitching, mild tremor, pain in my left shoulder, some rigidity. Chalking it all up to an injury, I consulted a sports medicine specialist. He referred me to a neurologist, who diagnosed young-onset PD. At thirty years old, I was told that whatever else I should expect, I could probably only work for another ten years. This was my explosion. This was my life skidding horribly sideways. Unable to process what was happening at first, I went into denial. Refusing to disclose my medical situation to anyone but family, and covering the symptoms with medication, I was really trying to hide from myself. Things would only get worse before they got better, though I'm convinced they only got better *because* they got worse. Losing my father staggered me, and the diagnosis left me reeling. Wary of placing a burden on my family, I pulled in and started to isolate myself.

When we're coming off of an accomplishment, or a series of accomplishments, we have an idea of who we are and what we represent to the people around us. How would this new, diminished version of myself measure up to the expectations I had for myself and my family?

Instead of coming up with new ways to deal with a new problem, I resorted to old coping mechanisms. From the time I was a teenager, through my early days in Los Angeles, to the heady days when my film and TV career was taking off, I'd always use alcohol as a sort of insulation. Strange as it seems now, I thought booze kept me sane: *I'd rather have a full bottle in front of me than a full-frontal lobotomy.* I never thought of it as a tool or a way of self-medicating; it was just part of the celebration. But what I was really doing was trying to soothe my anxiety and create a buffer between myself and the harsher aspects of reality. In my first year of living with Parkinson's disease, I took the buffer concept to a new extreme. If I couldn't obliterate the problem, I would obliterate myself, or at least my awareness of what was happening. Parkinson's medication for the symptoms, alcohol for the feelings; it didn't take long for this self-prescription to produce toxic side effects.

Before I continue with my own personal story, let me give you some idea of where I'm heading. It's all about control. Control is illusory. No matter what university you go to, no matter what degree you hold, if your goal is to become master of your own destiny, you have more to learn. Parkinson's is a perfect metaphor for lack of control. Every unwanted movement in my hand or arm, every twitch that I cannot anticipate or arrest, is a reminder that even in the domain of my own being, I am not calling the shots. I tried to exert control by drinking myself to a place of indifference, which just exacerbated the sense of miserable hopelessness.

I always find it ironic when people refer to me and my situation as "the fight of his life," or describe me as a "battler" or "engaged in a struggle." None of these terms apply to the way that I now approach my disease. The only way I could win—if winning means achieving and maintaining a happy and balanced life—was to surrender, and I took the first baby steps toward that victory by admitting powerlessness over alcohol.

Sober didn't mean better, not right away. Far from it. There were periods of time when I spent hours and hours submerged in the bathtub, a sort of symbolic retreat back to the womb. When I wasn't just trying to keep my head below water, the rest of those first couple of years without drinking were like a knife fight in a closet. With no escape from the disease, its symptoms, and its challenges, I was forced to resort to acceptance. A piece of wisdom I picked up along the way became the basis of a liberating new approach to life: "My happiness grows in direct proportion to my acceptance, and in inverse proportion to my expectation."

Obviously, I'm not suggesting that it's as easy as finding a switch marked "acceptance" and, by flipping it, flooding the problematic areas of life with edifying light. Would that we could. Acceptance, as I've come to understand it, simply means acknowledging the reality of a situation, that its truth is absolute. There's that word again. You may remember that I'm on record, going back to my school days, complaining to my mother about the stubborn intractability of mathematic absolutes. But I think I've finally figured out how two plus two can equal five. Or maybe—stick with me on this one—the precise equation is actually two *minus* two equals five.

The fallout from my father's death, the impact of a neurological illness, the emotional struggles and social isolation brought on by both my overuse of alcohol and the difficulties in giving up drinking: I first viewed all of these as setbacks. In her book *On Death and Dying*, Swiss psychiatrist Elisabeth Kübler-Ross broke down the process of death into five stages: denial, anger, bargaining, depression, and acceptance. I wasn't dying. Well, at least not anytime soon. But I was experiencing a profound sense of loss, and I came to understand that the Frau Doctor was incredibly astute. Denial: *This isn't happening.* Anger: *It's not fair.* Bargaining: *What can I do to get out of this?* Depression: *I can't, it's hopeless.* Acceptance: *What do I do now?*

It all came down to choices. As it related to the central issue of my life, I realized that the only choice *not* available to me was whether or not I had Parkinson's. Everything else—how much I understood about the disease, its emotional effect, its treatment, and its impact on my career and family—was up to me. In the short term, there's no doubt that any loss creates a void, a hole. My first instinct was to try to fill that hole in whatever way I could. To this end, I brought into play my ego, my will, and my own biased view of the ideal reality.

As my acceptance grew, I came to understand that loss is not a vacuum. If I don't impulsively try to fill the space it creates, it gradually begins to fill itself, or at least present choices. By choosing to learn more about the disease, I made better choices about how to treat it. This slowed the progress and made me feel better physically. When I felt better physically, I was happier in my surroundings, and less isolated, and could restore my relationships with my family and friends. Tracy, relieved that I not only was closer to the man she married but now an improved version, felt comfortable about expanding our family. And so Sam was soon joined by twin sisters, and in time, yet another sibling. Realizing that a film career that often sent me far from home for extended periods of time was no longer tenable, and accepting that I might only be able to work another ten years or so, I chose to make them ten good years and return to television.

Signing up for *Spin City* and choosing to film it in New York, where my family was based, not only was a great creative experience, but set me up well financially for a life in which my ability to ply my trade might understandably be limited. When that time came, I felt comfortable sharing my situation, not only with my circle of friends and associates, but with the public at large. Freeing myself from this isolation unleashed a flood of good will, and inspired me to capitalize on that good will to the benefit of the Parkinson's community. This led to the formation of the Michael J. Fox Foundation for Parkinson's Research, and in the decade since its inception—all credit to the dynamic and diligent group of people who signed on to carry out our mission—we've funded nearly 200 million dollars in cutting-edge research and, in many ways, created a new approach to the way cures are sought, here in America and around the world.

As promised, I've tried to avoid offering advice, per se. My intention in writing this book was to be illustrative, not prescriptive. However, let me make this suggestion: Don't spend a lot of time imagining the worst-case scenario. It rarely goes down as you imagine it will, and if by some fluke it does, you will have lived it twice. When things do go bad, don't run, don't hide. Stick it out, and be scrupulous in facing every part of your fear. Try to be still. It will take time, but you'll find that even the gravest problems are finite—and that your choices are infinite.

You may have heard me say this before, but I'll continue to repeat it until I find it not to be true: Because Parkinson's demanded of me that I be a better man, a better husband, father, and citizen, I often refer to it as a gift. With a nod to those who find this hard to believe, especially my fellow patients who are facing great difficulties, I add this qualifier—it's the gift that keeps on taking . . . but it *is* a gift.

Believe me, I still have the occasional fantasy that I'll wake up one morning, and as I begin to go about my day, gradually realize that I'm symptom-free. There's no tremor, no cramping, no shuffling, no pain. Having long ago accepted the realities of PD, the neurogenerative deterioration, the irreversible cell death, I know that, absent the discovery of a cure, it could never happen.

Except that it did.

If this sounds like a fairy tale, then the setting couldn't have been more appropriate: the mysterious and enchanting mountain kingdom of Bhutan. Nestled in the Himalayas, its rich Buddhist culture is alive in the sateen rainbow of the distinctive native dress, in the architecture, best described as a chalet/pagoda hybrid, and most expressively in the beaming faces of the Bhutanese people, young and old.

I was in Bhutan shooting footage for a documentary on optimism for ABC. Conceived as a companion piece to my book *Always Looking Up*, the film aimed to seek out people, places, and things that, in some way, represented the power of positive thinking. We had already traveled to Washington, D.C., for Barack Obama's inauguration, visited a cooperative dairy farm in upstate New York, and attended the Cubs' Wrigley Field home opener in Chicago. But it was our journey to the other side of the planet, with its water-color flora and fauna and soaring Himalayan peaks, shrouded in a wispy, diaphanous gauze of mist, that provided the emotional and philosophical heart of the piece. What compelled me to bring our crew here was the tiny kingdom's progressive trade policy and, really, their national ethos, built around a policy their king and government have labeled Gross National Happiness. In a world where most nations would seemingly go to any lengths to increase their Gross National Product, the Bhutanese believe that economic development should never come at the cost of their people's happiness. Therefore, in every trade deal the government enters into (for example, the sale of hydroelectric power to neighboring India), culture is valued more than cash.

Whatever steps have been taken to preserve the happiness and lifestyle of the Bhutanese people, it's very clear to the visitor that it's working. The country is both a monarchy and a democracy, and I spoke to many who expressed a love for their home and a gratitude to their king and countrymen. All due respect to Uncle Walt, but this is the true Magic Kingdom, the mythical Shangri-La made real. And that leads me to the part of the story that I alluded to earlier.

By the second day in the country, I noticed a marked diminishment of the kind of symptoms I generally wake up to every day. They eventually reappeared shortly after breakfast, but only very mildly, and it was well past noon before I felt compelled to take any L-Dopa (PD meds). Over the next few days, we traveled in and around the countryside, to schools and government buildings, farms and festivals, and while I wouldn't say that PD was completely gone and I was back to normal (if I can even remember what normal felt like), something was definitely happening. I waded through rice paddies, sat cross-legged for hours while taking a meal with local families, and wandered through Thimphu's crowded marketplace, investigating the myriad sights, sounds, and smells. I was able to do all this in inexplicably effortless fashion.

On the penultimate day of the trip, our producers and camera crew scheduled a demanding three- to four-mile hike up a local mountain to film one of Bhutan's most important religious sites, a monastery they call "Tiger's Nest." Originally, the idea was to capture background footage, what we call "B-roll," but I surprised myself by volunteering to come along. A week earlier, the prospect of successfully completing such a hike would have been optimistic even for me, but the physical change in me had been that dramatic.

Armed with a walking stick and accompanied by my intrepid guide, Tshewang, I set off on a slow and steady pace up the steep, winding trails. Just short of the monastery site, a flutter of prayer flags announced a small teahouse clinging to the mountainside. One of our cameramen trained his lens on me, and I related, for the documentary, my happy bewilderment at what I had done and how I had been feeling during my time in the Himalayas. Maybe it was the altitude that had brought about this change, or perhaps it was the medicine that I had been given to prevent altitude sickness. Whatever it was, I was grateful, though I had no delusions that it would remain that way once I returned to the States.

On my descent, in an act of hubris inspired by my improved sense of balance and fluidity, I strayed from the marked trails and attempted a shortcut down a ninety-degree rock face. Overwhelmed by momentum, I found myself skittering down the mountainside, toward certain injury and possible death. Flashback to Mexico—only now I had the advantage of being sober. Or was it a disadvantage? Flinging myself sideways to the ground seemed the only sure way to arrest my progress. Somehow I managed the maneuver. This little flurry of excitement resulted in scrapes, bruises, and a bloodied and mangled finger.

The next day, we flew to India to make our connection back to the States, and on the plane, I noticed something disturbing. I hadn't been able to remove my wedding ring because of the swelling, and now the cabin pressure was causing the digit to balloon and discolor even more. The wedding band was constricting to the point of strangulation. An Indian doctor, sitting in the row across the aisle, calmly informed me if I didn't cut that ring off in the next couple of hours, they'd be cutting off my finger. And so I made a detour to the hospital in New Delhi, and after a frantic search for the correct cutting implement, the ring was removed, the finger was saved, and I was on my way home.

Almost immediately upon my return to the U.S., the Parkinson's symptoms returned, and it was as if that mysterious and magical reprieve had never happened. But of course, it did. I carry a reminder with me every day. I only have to look down at my homely and still-misshapen ring finger on my left hand.

Of course, I also have a filmed record of the entire trip. Personally, I didn't take a single photograph while I was there, but that's not all that unusual for me. I suppose my aversion to snapping pictures may have something to do with shaky hands and blurry results, but there's another reason: The act of lifting up the camera and positioning it between me and the object of my interest separates me from the experience. The memory exists on photo paper, or is stored digitally and ready for download, but the emotional resonance is lessened. It may sound strange, but I know by the time I fumble out a camera (okay, PD definitely doesn't help), point, and shoot, I'm out of the moment. And if there's one basic lesson I've learned—in fact, kids, I think this is what it all boils down to—it is the cardinal importance of this moment . . . right now.

I'm not suggesting we wander around slack-jawed and stupefied, stumbling from moment to moment without a process that takes into consideration history or the future. Still, what's happened before and what may happen later can't be as important as what's happening now. There's never a better time to celebrate the present. The present belongs to you.

If you're a recent graduate or just being fitted for the robe, I'm sure there's no shortage of people who played a part in bringing you to this moment, and who may have an interest in where you go from here. It's reasonable. Parents, mentors, and friends are a part of your story, just as you're a part of theirs. They have hopes and dreams that may echo or overlap your own. And there's no reason why you can't make room for them. But what's happening to you right now, precisely at this instant, belongs only to you.

Own it.

Recovering alcoholics have an expression: "If you have one foot in yesterday and one foot in tomorrow, you're pissing all over today." With all that's happened, it's been liberating to understand that I don't have to carry the weight of all my disappointments or expectations. Sometimes it just is what it is. I can accept that.

This is your moment. Let someone else take the picture . . . just smile.

THE BEGINNING ... FINALLY

COMMENCEMENT ADDRESSES USUALLY WRAP UP WITH some broad sweeping statements about what to expect along the wide open road that stretches out in front of you. I'd love to do that, but I am not familiar with the stretch of highway you'll be traveling. I can only pass along notes from the route I've traveled. Forgive me for another gratuitous *Back to the Future* reference, but I can almost hear some of you out there rejecting the road analogy altogether: "Roads? Where we're going, we don't need roads!"

For a long time, as a high school dropout I considered my education to be incomplete, riddled with holes, gaps to be filled by lessons I hadn't shown up to receive. One crucial bit of wisdom that I did arrive at eventually was this: One's education is never complete. A missed opportunity doesn't preclude the possibility of new opportunities, or even better ones.

I think I benefited from being equal parts ambitious and curious. And of the two, curiosity has served me best. It's all very well to be absolutely certain, as I was when I dropped out of high school, about what you want to achieve or where you want to be in life. That's ambition. That's great. But nobody gets a straight shot to the top. Life is not linear. There will be detours along the way. For the curious, new clues will await at every turn and may keep pointing toward the chosen destination. Or maybe you'll stumble upon information that will inspire you to change course altogether, delivering you to a future you never could have imagined.

I credit my curiosity, in fact, with rescuing me from the edge of an abyss. Initially, my anxiety and confusion over my diagnosis of early onset Parkinson's disease had shut me down, and I felt overwhelmed by the desire to withdraw, to retreat from my situation. Once I accepted reality—*It is what it is*—my curiosity took over. I started to ask very simple questions. *What is Parkinson's, exactly? How is it affecting me? How is it affecting others?* And the scope of my inquiry widened: *Does this change how I feel about myself? Does it change how others feel about me? Does that really matter? Is what anyone else*

thinks of me really any of my business? Who are these
Parkinson's patients that make up this community I find
myself a part of, and what can I learn from them? Can we
do something to help ourselves? Can I personally do some-
thing?

You see where this detour led. Curiosity may have
killed the cat, but it saved my ass. When you move out of
your comfort zone and interact with people you might not
have otherwise, the results can be compelling. I'm thinking about the scientists I've met during my work with the
Michael J. Fox Foundation for Parkinson's Research. I
remember being briefed once by an esteemed clinical re-
searcher on the potential use of trophic factors in neurological repair. After admitting that I didn't understand a
word of what he just said, I told him, "If I'm in a room full
of actors, odds are I've got a pretty good shot of being one of
the smartest people in the room. But if I'm in a room full
of neuroscientists, I think it's best if I just nod and take
notes." Truth is, in a span of maybe a couple of years, I had
gone from talking to my agent on a cellular phone to dis-
cussing brain chemistry with cellular biologists.

Like I said, I'm not much for advice. But I'll leave you
with a quick review. Being in control of your own destiny

is a myth—and wouldn't be half as much fun anyway. Pay attention to what's happening around you. Read the book before you see the movie. Remember, though you, alone, are responsible for your own happiness, it's still okay to feel responsible for someone else's.

Live and learn.

—Michael J. Fox
New York City